THE INVISIBLE WOUND

THE INVISIBLE WOUND

"Living With Post Traumatic Stress Disorder"

THOMAS ALAN WERKHEISER
and
JILLENE KAE WERKHEISER

To order additional copies of this book, contact:
Xlibris Corporation
1-888-795-4274
www.Xlibris.com
Orders@Xlibris.com
56364

Contents

DEDICATION

This book is dedicated to the thousands of trauma survivors, both men and women, who have Post Traumatic Stress Disorder. The spouses and significant others of those afflicted are noted as well.

A special dedication in memoriam of Scott Leopold and Aaron Patterson, Vietnam veterans no longer with us due to the ravages of PTSD. They were fellow patients of mine in a PTSD program at American Lake Veterans Hospital, Tacoma, Wa., in 1986.

Life with PTSD

Days of sun filled with showers,
here I hide and lie away the hours.
A cloud of tears and still I see,
this is part of life with PTSD.

A crowd of people though still alone
consumed by dread, the ring of the telephone.
An encounter, do I fight or flee,
a part of the life with PTSD.

Intrusive thoughts come and go,
from where and why, I really don't know.
Eaten by depression, anger, anxiety
a certainty of life with PTSD.

Sleepless nights with vivid dreams
flashbacks by day, real as it seems.
Lord, please rid me of this misery
such is life with PTSD.

Longing for fellowship with other men,
search for a child's joy yet once again.
Realize in time, whatever must be
this is the life with PTSD.

by Thomas A. Werkheiser

This two part, self-help handbook describes in living color what it is like to live with post traumatic stress disorder. Although the accounts are given from a war veteran's perspective, the survivor of a severe trauma such as attempted murder, rape, or serious auto accident would have relativity to this book. The second part, co-authored by the victim's wife, conveys a detailed analysis of what life is like living with someone who has PTSD.

The symptoms of this incurable disease are discussed including triggers, depression, anger, nightmares, and flashbacks. Also cited, are examples of how these symptoms impact one's daily life.

Several excellent books have been written on PTSD from a clinical point of view. This book's perspective on the disease is given by two people living with it on a twenty-four, seven basis.

The book offers the reader signs to look for as to whether they or a loved one has PTSD. Additionally, outlets of where to go for help are discussed.

Part One

A Self Portrait of PTSD

by

Thomas Alan Werkheiser

Introduction

"Rejoice, O young man in thy youth"
Ecclesiastes 11:9

Post Traumatic Stress Disorder is a disease. *THERE IS NO CURE.*

T he purpose of this book is to alert and identify the causes and symptoms of post traumatic stress disorder (hereafter referred to as PTSD). This is purely from a victim's point of view rather than a sterilized, clinical expose by a doctor or other professional in the medical field. I have no doubt there will be those who will disagree or even disavow what I have to say. That's all fine with me. I have no desire to be portrayed as the bearded man atop the hill having all the answers about PTSD. This is my story.

My deepest gratitude goes to my wife who has greatly supported my efforts to write this book. Indeed, she has walked with me the past twenty-four years with PTSD in living color. With her wealth of experience, I have asked her to write Part Two "Spouses and Significant Others". I felt her input would have a broader impact on how loved ones must interrelate and identify with the person who has PTSD.

I have lived with this disease at least since I was diagnosed in 1986, seventeen years after I left Vietnam. I have a feeling that I became ill with it while I was still "in country" although I didn't realize it at the time. My life has been a rollercoaster ride of good and bad days ever since. By that I mean this disease can affect you with severe mood swings from feeling okay to ugly and back in the course of a day. There is medication to help with these mood swings but not to eliminate them.

When I began to write this book I had an idea it would be difficult to do, to say the least. It has proven to be a painful process. Describing PTSD forces me deep into an inner hell. Every element has brought forth mind numbing, gut wrenching, and tear jerking thoughts I had thought would be stuffed deep inside for all eternity. If not spurred on by my wife and several others, it probably would not have happened. All involved have stated this is something needed to be said.

To be clear, the clinical definition of PTSD as defined in the Merck Manual is "an anxiety disorder caused by exposure to an overwhelming traumatic event, in which the person later repeatedly reexperiences the event".

Whether PTSD is a disorder or an incurable disease depends on who you talk to. I prefer the latter since I have been told by professional clinicians that what I have won't go away. My preference is to find ways to live with it rather than be locked away or to end it all. Not to be coarse, my heart goes out to family and significant others of those no longer with us. I, too, have lost two dear friends since the war to this disease.

My PTSD all stems from combat related events in the Vietnam War. To be sure, any life threatening trauma, e.g. serious motor vehicle accidents, attempted murder, rape, and earthquake or hurricane victims would suffer from PTSD.

Many people afflicted with this disease from war experiences do not comprehend its magnitude. You are not a "monster". As you will see, there are several components, each of which can be debilitating to a "normal" lifestyle. Each component can and does interrelate. For example, a person with anger issues most likely has bouts of depression along with sleep-suffering nightmares. Some will have characteristics of one or two symptoms more prevalent than others. Hopefully, by better understanding the parts one can come to deal with the disease to bring about a healthier lifestyle. Similarly, a significant other can understand a loved one's affliction better.

A word about the title. More than a few veterans returning from Vietnam have agreed with me that something felt missing. That missing something turns out to be our inner self. You go through the motions of what seems like "life". The scars are physically unseen by others. Thereby exists the title, *THE INVISIBLE WOUND*.

Chapter One

Triggers

A trigger is anything, or perhaps anyone, that serves as a reminder of the trauma's events. Movies, magazine/newspaper articles, books, discussions, and television programs all fall under this category. A reminder may transform itself into the veteran's psyche either immediately or sometime later. The trigger usually manifests itself in the form of anxiety, depression, anger, or a combination of these symptoms. Another potential trigger is an anniversary date which would be the day a particular traumatic event took place such as a nasty firefight in a war.

I mentioned earlier that a person could be a trigger. I personally had a deeply troubling experience in Vietnam searching a sampan for contraband while I was on riverboats. We had lost two crewmen on other boats in the previous week, killed while on this type of duty so everybody was fairly keyed up. Among the Vietnamese on this sampan was an old woman chewing beetlenut which stained her teeth red. Beetlenut can act as a drug giving the user a high. As we lined these people up on their boat, the old lady was squatting and rocking back and forth. While rocking, she kept up this hideous laugh. I mean this woman was "dinkydow" or crazy. She kept staring at me with her continual cackle. This episode lasted until one of the other crewmen spotted a guy below deck with a gun. We wasted everyone on board and then lit fire to the sampan. To this day, if I hear a lady laugh similar to that old woman, it serves as a trigger for me.

While a in-patient in a PTSD program in 1986, I relived this experience in a focus group one day. The next day I am sitting in a classroom listening to one of the nurses talking about something calm and completely separate from the previous day's events. Suddenly, I had a flashback of this old woman which startled me so that I pushed my chair back a few feet and damn near fell on the floor. It lasted just a few moments but had a paralyzing effect on me the rest of my day. Once again, a trigger can have a delayed reaction without any warning.

During the same in-stay, a couple of the vets in my group decided to try to teach me how to play golf one afternoon. After teeing off, the three of us were walking down the fairway somewhat separated from each other. Without warning, I dove to the ground and didn't move for a few minutes. The other two guys came running over to me asking what happened. I told them I had a vision of being back on a riverboat in the middle of a jungle-lined river. The fairway lined by trees briefly became my Vietnam all over again. Needless to say, that ended my golfing experience.

The best way I know of in dealing with triggers is to avoid them as much as possible. Even a movie with violence having to do with your trauma should be viewed with caution.

Chapter Two

Numbing

Returning from the Vietnam War, my missing inner self could be termed as my loss of true personality. I knew it wasn't there anymore but I could not put my finger on why.

It seems this all started *before* I came home. I believe your mind has a built in shut down valve that kicks in when a severe trauma exposes itself. In my case, that valve operated when I was in my first firefight. It continued to operate with each firefight and mortar attack happening throughout my tour in Vietnam. This shutdown mode really helped blackout the normally horrific reaction to the screams and seeing guys shot or your buddy's arm getting blown off. That valve seemed to kick in more quickly as successive traumas took place.

This shutdown or numbing process continued right on home. It seems after it had operated several more times it didn't know how to shut itself off. I felt like I had turned into some kind of zombie. My girlfriend, at the time, would be ecstatic about having a fabulous day at work and my ho hum reaction would put her down in a heartbeat.

Most people upon getting hired at a new job would feel on top of the world. For me, it was just a relief that I could pay my bills. Thirty-eight years later nothing has changed. I feel I have to put on a Oscar award-winning performance to show a reaction that would be an automatic one for most people. When I still held a job, a normal process of getting ready for work in the morning was an ordeal in itself. I had no desire to go to work other than knowing I had no other way to pay the bills. Once at work, it was go through the motions to do the job without any self-satisfaction. I constantly fought with myself to break out of this "trance" that I would feel exhausted by noontime.

A typical evening was spent out until late drinking and shooting pool. Interaction with other guys was limited to the day's events and not much else. If they didn't know I was a "Nam" vet, so much the better. I absolutely never wanted to talk about my war experiences. I rarely dated. When I did, it was comprised of going out to dinner or a movie. I felt like a rookie out on the first date of his life. I never considered myself to be a sex maniac not that it wasn't important. You could say that I did have a below average sex life compared to some other guys. The girls I was attracted to wanted to form long term relationships which I didn't feel ready for. I couldn't figure out who I was so therefore I couldn't be there for a lady. One could sum things up by saying if you can't be there for yourself, you sure as hell can't be there for someone else.

Holding down a job proved to be such an ordeal that when I finally received a 100% service-connected disability rating from the Veterans Administration I thought I would be in seventh heaven. After a brief (and I do mean brief) initial euphoria, it was right back to the "just another day" routine.

I can't really say what it would take to break out of this mode because I honestly have no idea. I try to look for something each day to get relatively excited about to "bring me up". Sometimes it seems to work, most often it doesn't. I have tried to institute a thought process of visualizing at least one thing to look forward to doing or have happen each day. Sometimes it works. The danger of that is if it doesn't happen I rarely have a safety valve of something else to take its place.

Chapter Three

Depression

For me, depression is the worst symptom of PTSD. It seems to ooze from every pore in my body. I could safely say most all the other symptoms of PTSD have some relationship with depression.

When my depression manifests itself, my mind feels totally empty as if nothing matters. It is truly an exhausting behavior pattern draining me of whatever energy I have. Since my PTSD began to take shape in the early 1980's, I have literally fought depression every day of my life since.

The characteristics include a general unhappiness with life. Any and all positive feelings are viewed as only temporary and with distrust. There is no point in getting all warm and fuzzy inside when whatever happiness felt won't stay very long. I can remember when I was working a steady job, Monday through Friday, that on Friday I developed a general euphoria of the approaching weekend. By Saturday, though, that "high" was gradually being replaced with a growing letdown. Misery would settle in on Sunday knowing the next day it was back to work again. Generally, happiness is met with distrust since it lasts only a short time making it seem almost abnormal. A sense of doubt sets in the mind bringing an uncomfortable feeling to laughter and enjoyment of anything.

Depression can have a lasting effect on creating and maintaining friendships. There seems to be a tendency to retreat to your inner self. A certain comfort level is gradually achieved by a general avoidance of others. Normal communication skills start to break down from easy flow conversation to a necessary dialogue. You feel uncomfortable even around people you have known for a long time before the trauma existed. Staying home is the norm now instead of visiting familiar places with friends. Casual conversation with acquaintances or the cashier in the grocery store is limited to only what is necessary. Obviously, meeting new people and developing friendships is almost completely nullified. I can safely say I have made great efforts to avoid people many times. Body language says everything without uttering a word. It's like displaying a permanent "no vacancy" sign. When you walk into a waiting room at a doctor's office, you look for a chair apart from anyone else. When walking anywhere, you avoid eye contact or generally look down.

Family ties become strained or gradually, in some cases, disintegrate. PTSD cannot be underemphasized when it comes to this area of life. For family members that were around you before the trauma, you are in some ways two different persons, before and after. That fun loving social animal you were before is not there anymore. It is documented in my VA medical records in 1970, a social worker visited my mother while I was in the VA hospital. My mother told her "as far as I'm concerned, my son is dead". Bear in mind, I was not a convicted criminal but I resembled someone my mother did not know and didn't want to know. My father, even though he was a veteran of World War II and Korea, wasn't much help in trying to get her to understand. He essentially sided with my mom and I was, more or less, out the door. My older brother and I had a falling out as well. He had served in the Navy as a medical corpsman but avoided Vietnam due to his poor eyesight which I am thankful for. It has now been thirty-five years since I last saw my brother. I don't know where to locate him if he is alive or dead.

My wife, Jill, I found purely by chance twenty-four years ago. She worked as a manager of a coffee shop where I happened to stop into one night after the bars closed. We hit it off very well and six months later we were married. We have certainly had our ups and downs, twice separating for a short time but always finding the strength to reconcile. She had five children by a previous marriage and it was extremely difficult to learn fatherhood in a house full of teenagers. The kids viewed me skeptically as to whether I would run out on them or be a lasting influence. After this length of time, I am more or less accepted by them.

I have been lucky that Jill chose to take a real interest in my battles with PTSD. She has talked with a number of clinicians, read articles, and sought counselling to better understand the disease. It was only two years into our marriage when she had her first real taste of PTSD with me. In 1986, one night after work in a new job, I received a harassing telephone call from a bill collector. It left me severely depressed and in a very dark mood. Intrusive (negative) thoughts began to take hold of me. I became filled with malicious and suicidal ideations. Grabbing a butcher knife, I stood over the kitchen sink and plunged into a flashback. I was right back in Vietnam with everything I saw and felt. My wife, just having arrived home was very scared and called the police. When they came in the house, I turned and faced them with the knife uttering a mixture of profanities and Vietnamese. I was lucky that one of the cops was a Vietnam vet himself. He started talking to me and eventually got me to drop the knife. It's a good thing it wasn't some rookie who would probably have shot me. The police put me in their car and drove me to the main hospital with a psychiatric wing. While on the way there, the police had contacted my VA psych doctor, who claimed he hadn't seen me in a month. Actually, I had been to see him the previous week.

After a week at that hospital, I was transferred to the VA hospital at American Lake, in Tacoma, Wa., where I did the Thorazine "shuffle" for three months. My timing couldn't have been much better. I was then accepted into a fairly new three month in-patient PTSD program headed by Dr. Ray Scurfield at the same hospital. It was an excellent comprehensive program with courses ranging from Vietnamese history to intensive "focus" sessions which brought the reality of war back to the present with each vet member's recollections. Upon graduation, I felt capable of going right out and getting a new job. I was actually filled with a false sense of confidence that I had PTSD by its tail. If I had been able to receive better counselling upon returning home it would have been more advisable to have filed a claim with the VA for total and permanent disability due to axis one PTSD.

The problem with filing a claim with the VA is it takes up to a year or more to gain approval. The VA is constantly choked with claims as they have insufficient personnel and resources to action them. I felt pressure to gain prompt employment since my wife had "held down the fort" for the previous six months by herself. After finding a job, the following nine years were an inner hell. Trying to focus on maintaining good work performance while battling the ever present demons of PTSD was almost impossible. Finally, while at the local VA hospital for an appointment, I ran into a Disabled American Veterans counselor who told me she didn't think I could hold down a job much longer. She is the person who got me started on filing a 100% disability claim. Shortly thereafter, my boss at work let me go with a severance check. I had missed too many days at work and too often had yelled at other employees. The next year was a different kind of hell going through the claim process. From April, 1995 through to April, 1996, I had endured two government "shutdowns" and other bureaucratic holdups before being approved for total disability. My guilt-ridden depression over those twelve months drove me to tears on more than one occasion.

Depression breeds guilt over why I survived the war at all. Many times I have pondered the question of why did I come home while many others did not. From a religious standpoint, it is said God has a special purpose for survivors of trauma to accomplish other things. No concrete answer appears to be forthcoming to this open-ended question. Perhaps one answer is there are trauma veterans so that others will not forget the traumatic experience. To others, like myself, bearing this burden of guilt, the message may lie in living as fulfilling a life as possible.

Discomfort in my surroundings has led my wife and I to relocate several times in the past twenty-some years. The last time I checked my heritage I had no evidence of gypsy blood in me. But each time we have moved, I have felt okay for a few months then that comfort level begins to disappear. We have lived in the city, the country, then back to the city again. If we stay in the same place for a year or more it is a rarity. My wife has, more than once, asked me where I would be most happy. I can never seem to give her an intelligent answer. She says until you find peace within yourself, you will never be content. I believe she hit the nail on the head. That is just the problem. I have found it virtually impossible to find peace within myself. I definitely feel the war environment caused this behavior pattern. Under the threat of being attacked, I never felt comfortable in one place for very long. I realize that threat has ceased to exist, however, I cannot erase it from my mind.

When depression becomes severe, the thought of suicide occasionally rises to the surface. I have thought of committing suicide many times but only attempted it twice that I can recall. Both times consisted of overdosing a variety of pills and going to sleep. Fortunately, I woke up and continued on with my life. I am lucky to have a strong support base with my wife. If I was without her, I don't know if I would have the strength to carry on by myself. My faith in God is the ultimate safety valve I hold to keep from killing myself. Since the war, I have lost two Vietnam veteran friends to suicide. Without question, if you or a loved one has severe depression from PTSD, I cannot overestimate the value of having a strong support base of family, friends, and clinicians. Prescription medication for depression is strongly advised but, by itself, is not nearly enough to combat this symptom of PTSD.

Chapter Four

Anxiety and Anger

Severe fear or distress of unforeseen events is a legitimate form of PTSD. A trauma survivor can have difficulty handling anything other than the status quo. An anxiety sufferer exhibits a general nervousness when encountering anyone or anything that he or she considers abnormal.

Vietnam veterans commonly consider a "fight or flight" reaction to the unexpected. A quick deduction of the scenario, if hostile, will entail confrontation or getting the hell out of there. Virtually any encounter with anyone unknown triggers a general nervousness.

Combat veterans are uncomfortable in certain environments especially with crowds of people. These can range from a baseball stadium to a line at the grocery store. Anytime the vet has people behind him the discomfort level increases. When eating at a restaurant, the vet seats himself with his back to the wall. While in a queue at a business, the vet positions himself slightly sideways to be aware of anyone approaching from behind. If you are standing behind him in a line of people, believe me, it's much better to say something than to tap him on the shoulder.

People with PTSD have difficulty holding a train of thought. They are easily distracted and prone to forgetfulness. I can't count the number of times I have gone into a room and then I am unable to remember what I went in there for. If I have three or four things to do, my wife makes me write a list of what they are so I don't forget any of them.

Anxiety causes a great deal of stress. War veterans strive to be perfectionists. Mistakes by the vet or someone else are rarely tolerated. In war, a mistake can be life threatening and unfortunately, that line of thinking is carried home. Relations with family and friends can reach the breaking point for fear of errors in judgement.

As in other symptoms of PTSD, there are prescription medications available to help with severe anxiety disorder. If you suffer from this problem and are confronted with obstacles, my advice is to try and take a deep breath and sort out the best procedure before going forward. I can't guarantee that will work every time but it is worth the effort.

Like pain, anger is categorized on a one to ten scale. A person with PTSD can rise from a one to a ten in a heartbeat. Anger levels are difficult to control since they can increase rapidly. Of all the signs of PTSD, anger is the quickest to be realized. It is also the most common reaction to a variety of happenings including bad news, interruptions, abrupt changes in plans, mistakes, and general frustration.

It is easier for a person with PTSD to reach for anger than happiness. I believe this to be true because that person no longer has the ability to channel or process a low level of anger into a more constructive or peaceful state of mind. One reacts rather than thinking things out. With PTSD, if something can go wrong it most certainly will go wrong. For those having been in the military service that is especially true. Where else could the term "snafu" (situation normal, all fouled up) have arisen.

This is how a typical day with PTSD can go. First, the alarm doesn't go off, so you wake up late; already a level two of anger. As you race around the house trying to get dressed, you can't find a clean pair of matching socks. Now you've reached a level three. Having time for a quick bite, you pour a bowel of cereal and then realize there is no milk. You haven't even stepped out the door and you are already at a level four. As you warm up the engine of your car, the needle on the gas gauge is a hair above empty. Now you are pissed off a level six for not getting gas on the way home last night. Don't forget, being forgetful is a part of PTSD. After paying four dollars a gallon for gas, you have attained an anger level of eight. Two blocks from the appointment you are ten minutes late for, a guy cuts you off in traffic . . . level nine. After walking in the door, the secretary for the person you came to see says sorry, you must now reschedule the appointment it took you three weeks to get in the first place. Now at a level ten, you completely lose your temper and read her the riot act. Sometimes, all these steps don't happen; you can go from a "3" to an "8" at the snap of a finger. It all depends on the circumstances. Once you have reached a level eight, anything or anyone is fair game.

For me, as a combat vet, fear manifests itself in the form of anger. One might consider this to be abnormal to a normal reaction of being scared. I believe there to be different levels of fear. The most extreme level would be a person reacting with a "numbing" feeling. My perception is that after a person has experienced several life threatening episodes, he or she loses touch with normal reality. If you unexpectedly approach me from behind, I will most likely turn to hit you rather than jump away.

Anger associated with sufferers of PTSD creates very high stress levels and abnormally high blood pressure. A greater length of time is necessary to calm down. Perhaps a good way to deal with anger is to create a "safe zone" when you start to become edgy. This probably should be done beforehand. It can be a place that is quiet such as a backyard patio or a basement workshop away from the pressures of the day. As always, there are prescription medications available from your doctor that can help with anger control.

Chapter Five

Intrusive Thoughts

W ithout apparent forethought, negative conceptions push to the front of the mind. These impulses are instinctive without any apparent reason behind them. Intrusive thoughts are always "downers" that erase whatever positive feelings the person has.

Often these thoughts are referred to as mood swings that can happen in a flash. If you happen to be around other people at the time, they are startled at how quickly you can change from a good to a bad mood. Intrusive thoughts develop with a mental picture of a person or a thing. Usually it involves something a person said or a situation that took place earlier that day or possibly days ago.

I have been troubled by intrusive thoughts for several years. Since this symptom of PTSD is so prevalent in my daily life, it ranks at the top of all my problems associated with this disease. An example of an intrusive thought would be an argument I had last week with a family member. Now, most people would forget about it by the next day. For me, it doesn't go away. I could be in a decent mood several days later but if that person happens to stop by the house or telephone my wife, I immediately lapse into a bad mood. Another example might involve the monthly process of renewing my narcotic pain medication from the VA. Normally, a week before I run out of pills, my wife telephones a staff nurse at the VA to begin the procedure to have my doctor write the prescription which is then forwarded to the pharmacy to fill and mail out. One particular time someone did not get the prescription to the pharmacy to be filled. I ended up running out of pills. That put me in a world of hurt because I have severe lower back pain. After my wife made numerous calls to the VA, the order was filled but that entailed making a special trip to the hospital to pick them up. This rather than waiting more time for the pills to be delivered by mail. Now, every month I am consumed by an intrusive thought that a snafu will happen again.

As you can see from the above examples of intrusive thoughts, they can play a vital role with PTSD. A person has no control as to when an intrusive thought might arise. It may be a particular person, thing, event, or time of day that can set you off. If you think about it there is no rule of thumb or reason, it just happens.

Intrusive thoughts can ruin your hour, day, or month. You will have problems socializing with people, e.g. relatives, friends, doctors, or even your spouse. You gradually withdraw into your inner self causing depression, anxiety, and anger which are all parts of PTSD.

Can one control this? No. Anyone or anything is incapable of controlling intrusive thoughts. This is why they play such a vital role with PTSD. You are at the mercy of them which seem to rule your entire outlook on life. It stops you from having any positive form of existance in your daily structure of life. As said at the outset of this book, there is no cure for intrusive thoughts or PTSD as a whole. So much more could be said perhaps but actually there is no need to say anymore. I don't know of any medication or counselling that specifically addresses intrusive thoughts.

Chapter Six

Hyper-Vigilance and Startle Response

Hyper-vigilance involves an abnormal increased awareness of your environment. You feel a sensation of being "on watch" or guard duty. An unusual perception of happenings especially on your home turf takes place.

The security of family and personal possessions is paramount. You are overcome with a need to know the whereabouts of your wife and family members. Just like in the war environment, you set the boundaries of your property as your "perimeter". Personal articles such as your wallet, watch, and important documents are put in the same place at all times when not on your person. When you leave the house, every door and window must be shut and locked. I have been known to lock the front door, leave the house and come back sometimes two or three times to check that everything is okay.

My wife and I presently live next to an apartment complex on a busy street where there are people coming and going all the time. This only serves to heighten my vigilance which creates added agitation. The majority of people keep to themselves but it really doesn't matter. Generally, if there are people near my house that I don't know, I become irritated. This problem varies from moderate to severe depending on the time of day. Usually I don't become too upset during daylight hours.

As darkness approaches, my hyper-vigilance swings into high gear. This probably stems from Vietnam where the enemy had a propensity for attacking at night. I subconsciously tense up and become much more alert as it gets dark. Typically, I make sure the outside house lights are turned on and have only inside lights on that are necessary. It is easier to be seen from the outside if the rooms are well lit. Deadbolt and other security locks are set and checked periodically. If there is an unexpected knock at the door or the telephone rings after 10 p.m., I become alarmed. I also ensure that my guns are cleaned, loaded, and nearby just in case. On the other hand, I don't pace the floors with my revolver on my hip. But generally, I take nothing for granted.

This routine of hyper-vigilant activity certainly has its drawbacks. Not only do stress levels increase rapidly but it can definitely create a loss of appetite. Normal sleep patterns are non-existent. Without medication, I usually fall asleep out of pure exhaustion. I envy my wife who can get to sleep rather easily. All in all, I don't know how to relax having this disorder.

Startle response is characterized by a sudden hyper reaction to a loud noise or being surprised by someone or something. For example, you are walking down the street and a car backfires. Most people would probably just turn their head. For a war veteran, the reaction is to hit the ground. I can remember my Dad, a war veteran, telling me about that when I was a kid. At the time, I found it difficult to believe a person would react that way. After coming back from Vietnam, having witnessed numerous mortar and rocket attacks, I understood first-hand what he had talked about.

The other form of startle response entails a more violent reaction. If a person comes up behind me and taps me on the shoulder, I tend to turn and be ready to fight. The same holds true if I am awakened by someone touching me anywhere above the waist. My brother made that mistake after I came home from the war and I knocked him into the closet. My wife knows to shake my leg or foot to wake me up.

I wish I could say the passage of time has improved my disposition with this part of PTSD. Thirty-nine years later, I can't say that I have improved except to tone down my violent reactions. If its any help, I would suggest to those afflicted to discuss these problems with family and close friends to forge a better understanding.

Chapter Seven

Nightmares and Flashbacks

N ormally, nightmares are bad dreams experienced by most everyone. In the case of PTSD, nightmares take the place of the actual trauma realized by the victim. They can happen two to three times per week with an average of five years after the trauma took place. After that they lessen to perhaps once a week.

In the first few years, the nightmares are extremely vivid, recalling most, if not all, of the traumatic experience. For a war veteran involved in numerous hostile encounters, usually the most severe happenings are relived in the dreams.

My worst nightmare involves an attack from shore on my riverboat in August, 1969. We were on a routine night patrol just a few days before I was supposed to go home. As we rounded a bend in the river, we were hit by small arms fire and rocket propelled grenades. One of the RPG rounds hit the hull of the boat just aft of amidship cutting the boat almost in half. I was on the stern mounted M60 machine gun and the concussion catapaulted me into the air. I landed on my back, half in the boat and half in the water. A second boat came up and fished me out of the water. Two of our crewmen were killed. If not for the rescue, I am almost certain I would have been killed or taken by the enemy as a prisoner of war.

Several times after reliving these nightmares, I have awakened screaming or with the cold sweats. Once, I got out of bed and retreated to a corner of the dark room. I believe I stayed there in a crumpled mass for a couple of hours before I returned to bed.

Over time, these dreams have become cloudy in vision but can be just as intense. Fortunately, they don't occur nearly as often. There is medication available from your doctor that specifically targets nightmares. The pills have lessened the intensity and frequency of the dreams for me.

Flashbacks are vivid recounts of the trauma experienced while the person is awake. They are sudden reenactments that can occur without warning. Usually, they are triggered by something that reminds the person of the trauma such as a helicopter flying overhead or watching a movie or war documentary on television.

Flashbacks are hard not only on the victim but also very difficult for family, friends, and, most importantly, on the spouse. My wife will relate some strong examples in her part of the book on significant others. I will try to explain here what it is like for me.

First, the American Heritage Desk Dictionary defines a flashback, "to show or tell about an incident or scene from the past". This does not completely describe what happens. For those with PTSD, a flashback not only "shows" or "tells" of the past, it places you in the past. By this I mean your mind, not body, believes and thinks as if you are truly at the place of your flashback.

An example of this is the one particular flashback that put me in the VA hospital for six months. This was so real that I acted it out. I had talked about it in a previous chapter but I will explain how it really happened.

One night my wife had gone out leaving me alone with three of our five children. All of our five kids are from my wife's first marriage as, thanks to exposure to Agent Orange, I was unable to naturally father any children. I had had a stressful day at my new job so I was feeling angry and fearful of losing that job. The telephone rang and the kids were acting up. The caller was a bill collector who was rather nasty. I began getting angrier just as my wife came in the door. I was consumed with anger and depression. The next thing I knew, I was back in Vietnam with a flashback. I went into the kitchen, grabbed a butcher knife and stood in front of the sink. In my mind, I was back on the riverboat with the old, laughing Viet Cong woman who wanted to see me dead. My wife made the mistake of putting her hand on my shoulder to offer help. In a combination of Vietnamese and English, I yelled at her not to move or I would kill her as I held the knife to her throat. She yelled for the kids to call 911 for help. When the police finally arrived, one of them started talking to me. I later found out he had also been in Vietnam. He was able to calm me down before taking me to the hospital.

This example has caused a great deal of problems with the children growing up. They are still afraid of me, not knowing if that episode will happen again. I don't even know if it would happen again. This flashback has made it very difficult for my wife because the children, now adults, still don't like to come around very much. They can't get it out of their minds even though they realize I am much better now. I guess all of them fear of another flashback like that one.

Flashbacks cause mood swings as well. My wife's family has never understood this, thinking the worst of me. Many times I have gone into a different room or left the house when they come over. It is almost impossible to explain to them that it is the PTSD that causes the problem.

As a rule, flashbacks are extremely scary for all concerned and can last for several minutes to over an hour in duration. I strongly advise the person afflicted to avoid any triggers of the trauma he or she experienced. Again, like other components of PTSD, there is no cure for flashbacks.

Chapter Eight

Recognition of PTSD by the US Government

The US Government did not recognize PTSD as a disease, in of itself, until the 1980's. Prior to that, veterans returning home from wars with mental disorders were diagnosed with the labels of shell shock or battle fatigue. Care was given chiefly through individual counselling by a psychiatrist and a smattering of group discussions with a facilitator. Those with a moderate degree of disability were usually treated with a myriad of pills. More serious cases were given more powerful drugs such as Thorazine.

In 1970, after discharge from the service, I was diagnosed as having paranoid deficiencies along with battle fatigue. I was admitted into the VA hospital in Sepulveda, Ca., toward the end of 1970. I had knocked my brother through a glass shower door of the apartment we were sharing. He had been giving me a steady dose of verbal abuse because I had lost my job. I just snapped and went after him. He said I was nuts and needed to be "put away". The next thing I know, my brother had called a taxi to take me to the VA hospital. I was so agitated on the trip that the cab driver kept an eye on me in the rear view mirror wondering if I was going to go off on him.

At the hospital, I was assigned a psychiatrist who prescribed several types of pills and had individual sessions with me. I felt like a lab rat with all the pills I was taking. They put me in a ward with several other veterans of different wars. Typically, World War II and Korean War vets didn't think much of us who had served in Vietnam. They belittled the war and those of us who fought in it as insignificant. Needless to say, there was a fair amount of dissension existing on a daily basis.

One day, a Korea vet and I got into a dispute over a game of dominoes. He said some nasty things to me and then I took off after him. He ran and locked himself in a small coffee room about the size of a large closet. I completely lost it trying to rip the door off the hinges. It ended with six orderlies trying to subdue me. The nurse gave me an injection of something that put me in a stupor. I was then shipped up to the locked ward where I stayed for three months. My doctor put on Thorazine which made me like a zombie. I did the "Thorazine" shuffle for a few weeks.

I was transferred back to the "open" ward which again consisted of individual sessions with the doctor and a few groups. Fortunately, it wasn't twenty years earlier when I would have arrived back after being given a lobotomy or electro-shock therapy. When finally discharged, I was given some pills and told to be on my way. It was back to facing the world with not much going for me than when I had gone into the hospital.

Without a doubt, the best care I have received for PTSD was the in-patient program I attended in 1986. The program was headed by Dr. Ray Scurfield and lasted for three months. Everything from proper nutrition to a history of Vietnam to focus groups was covered. There were also combat veterans on staff available for individual counselling as needed twenty-four hours a day.

During the 1980's while Ronald Reagan was the president, the VA appeared to receive a sufficient budget to allow for good caliber programs. Unfortunately, in the 1990's and since, the VA has had inadequate budget funding causing a significant drop in quality programs for PTSD. I attended two short stay (one week) follow-up programs in the 1990's in which more than half the classes were cancelled due to insufficient staffing. I know there are a great number of veterans of Iraq and Afghanistan who are in dire need of good quality care. I have never understood the government's ability to send young men and women into multiple hostile deployments without having necessary care for them available upon their return home.

It is important to note that any person's life, whether they have PTSD or not, is governed as to how their physical well being affects their mental well being and visa versa. For example, if that person must deal with chronic physical pain, that in turn, will directly affect their mental outlook on life.

In the thirty-eight years I have been in the VA system, I have never understood why they treat the physical and mental parts as two separate issues. I surely know that the acute back pain I have suffered since Vietnam directly affects my psychological outlook on life. I have had three lower back surgeries in the past eight years and now I am told there is nothing, other than narcotics, they can do to relieve my pain. Unquestionably, this has a direct bearing on my PTSD dealing with depression and anger. As a result, I am much more inactive than I should or could be. Rarely, do my wife and I, as a couple, socialize with family and friends. I am more apt to spend my life at home, with my wife or alone, than to go out and try to enjoy life. It is unfortunate that the VA believes in a policy of dispensing medication rather than counselling which is provided on a limited basis.

Conclusively, the federal government has let down the young men and women they have turned into veterans. In all the wars fought by this country, the government has liberally sacrificed the lives of its young people and not legitimately taken care of those left alive. Maybe it should be the politicians who should fight the wars. The Congressional men and women, as well as the President, should shoulder the blame as to why adequate resources are not supplied to care for all veterans, as well as those suffering from PTSD. Countless families have sons, daughters, brothers, sisters, mothers, and fathers whose lives have been ripped apart by PTSD. As an example, at least ninety-five per cent of all marriages of Vietnam veterans with PTSD have ended in divorce. I remain convinced if not for the pressure on the federal government applied by service organizations like the Disabled American Veterans, we, as veterans, would not have the level of care we receive today. Finally, my heart goes out to those men and women who are presently on waiting lists for care by the VA after their tours of service have ended.

Chapter Nine

Living in the USA

Generally, the American society doesn't know what PTSD is. Presently, countless men and women have been diagnosed with the disease acquired from service in Iraq and Afghanistan. Even if a family member is afflicted with PTSD, most Americans do not understand its effects. They just see that their loved one is not the same person before he or she went overseas.

Before Vietnam, Americans were conditioned that we won our wars. Those who came home psychologically scarred were taken care of quietly or, at the worst, put away in an asylum. Our country's interventions into Vietnam and now Iraq and Afghanistan have been met by open hostility and disbelief by its people. Those who suffer from PTSD have been forced to keep it virtually to themselves. After all, the USA has not been invaded since the War of 1812. The American people generally do not comprehend the traumas experienced by other countries from invasion and occupation. They expect those who have fought battles to come home and blend back into society as if nothing ever happened.

During the Vietnam War, some soldiers came home and burned their uniforms amidst all the turmoil here at home. At the very least, we, as Vietnam veterans, didn't talk about having been over there, in public. Those with PTSD did more damage to themselves by "stuffing" their inner emotions. Unquestionably, the characteristics of PTSD are exacerbated by the veteran's inability to discuss his feelings openly. Some Americans even referred to the vets as "losers" and "baby killers". Even the Veterans of Foreign Wars clubs denied them entrance. We were the wrong people being blamed for the war when actually the finger should have been pointed at the federal government for prosecuting the war.

The pot would boil over concerning the present interventions if the president reinvoked the draft. He knows the American people would have him tarred, feathered, and run out of town if he did that. Instead, he deploys limited troops, reservists, and the state's national guards overseas for multiple tours of duty. Simply put, these young men and women are being put in harms way too often. As a result, many are now afflicted with PTSD while several have committed suicide.

Americans are a proud and just people. They basically want what is best for this country. The people seek to forget about Vietnam and its participants but mystifyingly allow their government to meddle into Iraq, in some ways a mirrored image of Vietnam. Perhaps I am an idealist but I believe the people should demand that their politicians stop these interventions and take care of those who have fallen to the traumas of war.

The people tend to believe what the media reports or editorializes. The war in Vietnam appeared in print and on television as winable and close to ending until the Tet Offensive of 1968. Reports of military installations being attacked and, in some cases, overrun by the enemy initialized a negative bias against the war. The more this reporting continued the worse the resentment built, especially against the combat troops. Nightly pictures on television showing mangled, dead bodies of Vietnamese men, women, and children fostered a hatred by a growing element of American people against the soldiers. This negativity has left a lasting imprint, especially in the minds of those with PTSD.

Because of that negative bias by the media during Vietnam, the military brass tend to censor a greater portion of the news reports out of Iraq and Afghanistan. Grisly photographs of bloodied bodies are extremely limited. Thus, the American public is given a more sanitized, black and white version of the current conflicts.

Except for the occasional news documentary on television, PTSD is rarely covered in the media. Recently, a local newspaper reported on the growing number of cases of PTSD with veterans of Iraq and Afghanistan. But most people are unfamiliar with what it's all about. Apparently, PTSD is not considered as newsworthy enough to be more exposed to the viewer or the reader.

Movies have a long history of glamorizing war. When I was a kid, movies about World War II were commonplace, reverant, and in black and white. Actors such as John Wayne and Audie Murphy were depicted as honorable superheroes. The viewing public was left with a sense of war being righteous and noble.

This seemed to change when the comparably few movies about Vietnam were shown in the 1970's and 1980's. One, in particular, did a huge disservice to the veteran of that war. "Apocalypse Now" was a nauseating, surreal portrayal of supposed activities of the soldier and sailor in Vietnam. One scene shows a guy waterskiing behind a PBR (riverboat). I don't ever recall being in a position to do that. The problem is the viewing public tends to believe that if they show it on the silverscreen then that bullshit supposedly must have happened.

The Oscar-winning flick "Platoon" tried to depict the reality of war in some measure but it tended to romanticize the war to some degree. If a person wants to see some form of the vivid reality of war, try watching the first five minutes of "Saving Private Ryan".

For a veteran with PTSD, I would make a strong effort to avoid any movie about war. These flicks will only serve to aggravate the disease you have.

Chapter Ten

Sorting It All Out

Many of those who have PTSD live in some form of self-exile. They hibernate in their homes or, in some cases, hide out in the wilderness. The problems they have are considered by them too overwhelming to exist in the public domain. Even with the degree of help and medication I receive from the VA, rarely do I venture into public places. I realize that hermatizing myself is not the answer to my problems but I feel more comfortable in my home. Occasionally, my wife gets me out of the house when she runs errands or goes grocery shopping. I have an inner desire to want to go out for entertainment and perhaps meet new people. However, I have somewhat of a fear of being in public. I don't know how to overcome this phobia. Over the years I have developed a comfort zone with this lifestyle; one that I feel is gradually driving me into insanity. Thanks to PTSD, my self esteem is severely lacking.

I believe PTSD to be contagious. My dear wife having put up with me for the past twenty-four years, I am sure has some form of PTSD. She will discuss her feelings on this in Part Two of this book. PTSD rubs off, even on the pets. My four dogs and especially my African Grey parrot have some elements of PTSD. The bird mimics my coughs and sneezes and has a vocabulary that won't allow a church group to come to the house. When I get angry, the bird gets angry. I am not trying to make light of PTSD but sometimes in some absurd ways it can be comical. By the way, the parrot now five years old can live to be one hundred. That must be my legacy to future generations, whomever is lucky enough to inherit the bird.

Something I feel I share with other combat veterans is an intolerance for making mistakes. Whether a mistake is made by me or someone else makes no difference. I know this feeling is derived from the war I was in. Mistakes by anyone could cost lives. I took this feeling home with me and still remain the same. I try to make a honest effort to be as tolerant as possible since everybody, including me, does mess up from time to time. There is no doubt that I am more difficult on myself than others. When I make a mistake, I tense up and become angry. Usually, I have to take a time out from whatever I'm doing to gather my composure. I tend to get angry with others who make mistakes but the degree of my anger depends on what the problem is and if it could have been avoided. For example, if someone says they are going to call me at a certain time and then don't call, I really get upset. If they call later and explain why they didn't call, most likely I will let it be. If I promise something to someone and forget, I try to make an effort to make it right. Whatever it takes.

With PTSD, there is a terrible problem I have with guilt feelings. Many times I have wondered why I made it home alive and others did not. Survivor guilt, I am sure, affects many war veterans. I have talked with clergy, doctors, and other professionals about this difficulty and no one can offer a meaningful explanation. If I am having an exceptionally bad day, I have a tendency to drift into this thought process of guilt. Care must be taken or else a severe depression can develop. If you have survivor guilt, take time to discuss it with others. Perhaps you can make some sense out of it.

Another problem I have associated with PTSD is a fear of being "left behind". This, too, is a product of my tour in Vietnam. In Chapter Eight, I shared an experience when my boat was ambushed shortly before returning home. During the period I was in the water before being picked up by a second boat, I developed this fear. Again, it is something I took home with me. It manifests itself whenever I am home alone. My anxiety level increases dramatically. Often now as I get older, this fear takes over when I think of what might happen if my wife passed away. I honestly do not know how I would survive. Would I take my life or be able to find comfort with someone else? I am against suicide but on the other hand, at the age of sixty, I don't think it possible for another woman to share my life with PTSD.

As I said in the introduction, PTSD is a chronic, incurable disease. It can strike anyone who has undergone a serious trauma. I have written about it from the perspective of my trauma being a war veteran. Due to its character and several parts, I strongly advise those afflicted and their loved ones to find ways to live with PTSD. There are several medications and counselling help available to maintain a somewhat acceptable lifestyle.

I sincerely have designed and written this book not only to share my experiences but also to offer empathy for others. With our varied experiences with PTSD, it is the hope of both my wife and I that this book will be of some help to others.

Part Two

Spouses and Significant Others

by

Jillene Kae Werkheiser

Introduction

The Road Construction and Detours of Life

A s the wife of a Vietnam vet, I will try, in my own way, to help anyone walk down the rough and bumpy road to a somewhat paved one. If you think about it, our lives are always under construction. If I can help you get through all the detours and rough roads to a smoother road then I will feel my stress, anger, and depression was well worth it, even if it's only one person that I help.

Having been married for twenty-four years to my wonderful husband, I know all the construction, detours, and rough roads have been worth it. Just keep in mind any time there is construction, there is always an end to it. Keep the faith, be patient, and keep in mind the road does smooth out.

In Part Two of this book, I will try to help you through the battles for the person with PTSD, the spouses, and significant others. I will tell it in my own words to the best of my ability. In doing so, I hope to ease your pain and challenges of getting through the VA system. My private accounts are to help you understand some of the traumas and battles you must or may go through. It's not easy to write. It brings back some very bad memories but also some good times for it is always darkest before the dawn. Not everyone will go through so many problems as I have and I pray you don't.

The reasons my husband and I decided to write this book were 1) to face our ghosts and ease our pain in all the battles we have experienced and 2) to help even ONE person would make us feel a thousand times better. So get ready to witness the battles for him, myself, and the winning of them.

Chapter Eleven

The Battle for Him

If I had a dollar for every doctor my husband has seen, we might be RICH. You can't choose your doctor at the VA nor can you have a say in what type of doctor you see. The VA assigns you a doctor. By this I mean, they do not take the time to hear what you have to say or what your needs are. They just give you a general doctor and that's it, take it or leave it. When you are seen, they decide what needs you have.

When Tom started having problems with PTSD, that I was aware of, in 1985, we went to the VA hospital in Spokane, Wa., to see his regular doctor. He said it was just slight stress and put Tom on a light depressant pill. As time went on, Tom's "slight" stress grew to high stress, depression, and suicidal thoughts. We went back to the VA hospital and to yet a different doctor as the first one had left the system. This doctor upped Tom's medication and suggested Tom go to counselling at the Vets Outreach Center.

Tom started group counselling at the Outreach Center and it was a disaster waiting to happen. The groups were gripe sessions or it was one vet trying to outdo the other vets with stories. There was no control in the groups and no endings either. Tom would get so upset from the groups that sometimes driving home he would go through flashbacks, anger, and intrusive thoughts. You can't have vets telling stories without a closing time to the night. Finally, he gave up on the groups. They seemed to do more damage than good.

Tom grew angrier and more depressed. We went back to the VA hospital and told the psychiatrist about what happened in the groups. By the way, it takes almost a month to get appointments at the VA. What did the doctor do? He increased Tom's meds and suggested Tom go into the hospital for in-patient treatment. He felt Tom couldn't get along with anyone in the groups, at work, or with the doctors at the VA because of his anger issues. This really made a whole lot of sense coming from a doctor who wasn't a veteran himself and apparently did not understand PTSD. I could go on about the doctor problems, but I don't want to bore you in that department. All in all, we have spent probably several hundred hours at the VA and still no real help for Tom, at this time.

Now we are where PTSD is affecting his job. Tom must not only battle the VA system but he had difficulty on the job because of his severe PTSD problems. After battling for five plus years, he could no longer function in the work environment. We applied for 100% disability compensation from the VA as Tom could no longer work. The doctors, at the Spokane VA hospital, said there was nothing more they could do to really help Tom.

We went through two federal government shutdowns in 1995, and almost a year before Tom was granted 100% disability. He is now totally and permanently disabled from PTSD. During the time we waited for the government to come through, we had severe problems financially and with our marriage. I did all I could to keep the bill collectors away and feed the family with the jobs I was holding. The big problem was not my husband's lack of effort but the ability of the government to do the right thing and on a timely basis.

Now, Tom is trapped in his own world of PTSD with little or no help from the VA in dealing with it. Yes, he was granted 100% disability and gets paid for it but this, in no way, covers his problems with the disease. The anger, flashbacks, dreams, depression, and now the inability of being able to work or care for his family is just devastating to him. THANK YOU, UNCLE SAM!

My family is of no help for they, as well as so many other people, do not understand PTSD. Most people think the person with the disease is off balance and crazy, not sick. For anyone with PTSD, it is hard for spouses, family, and strangers to understand what is really wrong. It's easier to walk away or just not have anything to do with the person. My own mother never understood Tom. She always thought Tom was self-centered and cared only for himself. She always thought he had a great deal of anger problems. I would try to explain PTSD to her but, like so many people, she thought it was just an excuse. You have to understand that PTSD is like any other disease, in that, if you don't take the time to understand the whats and whys, you will not only hurt the person with it but also the person who is married to or living with them.

I strongly suggest if you care enough for anyone with PTSD, you do some research on it. This will help everyone involved, especially the afflicted one.

Chapter Twelve

The Battle For Me

I feel somewhat an expert on being married to Vietnam veterans with PTSD. I am not trying to make light or fun of a vet with PTSD. I am looking to give some insight to it. Having lived through five marriages, I have a few things to say that just might help you.

Four of my five husbands are veterans. It has not been easy to live with them. They are all different in how they perceive the war, as well as, what they did during the war. The latest VA report states only five per cent of one hundred women will stay married to a Vietnam veteran for more than three years. It's a hard life but well worth it when you find the right one. I know in my heart, for the past twenty-four years, I have.

My first was the father of all five of my children. He was in the Army. While in basic training, he hurt his back and was sent home. His guilt of not being able to go to Vietnam changed his view on life. He felt he let the other vets down because of medical reasons. His brother went on to fight in the war. To this day, in my heart, I think he still feels guilty for not doing his part and needs to move on.

My second husband was in the Navy. He was a gun controller on a huge ship. He was never on the ground in Vietnam but shot the big guns at certain targets per orders. He was discharged with a hearing loss and anger problems. This was due to shooting at unseeable targets and not knowing who or what he was shooting at. He could no longer perform his duties and was given a honorable medical discharge. They called it battle fatigue.

He chose to not seek help from the VA stating he was fine and to leave him alone. He drank about half to three quarters a bottle of whiskey sometimes every night to ease his pain, nightmares, and anger. He never would take orders and hated authority of any kind.

49

After about six years, his drinking got totally out of control. I pleaded with him to seek help from the VA. He refused and would angrily tell me I didn't know shit and slap me around. Like so many vets, he wouldn't admit there was a problem because he was in denial or ashamed and didn't want to face the issues. It was easier to become angry rather than face the problem. That way he could blame it on me and not deal with it.

One day, he came to me drunk and said he couldn't stand to be with me and my five bratty kids. He was leaving me. I tried to stop him and that was a mistake. He beat me and went out the door. I was so scared that I told the kids not to come out of their rooms. I hid in a corner of my bedroom and didn't move for fear of him coming back into the room and beating me again. I remember I would urinate in the corner of the room because I was so afraid. After that, I totally broke down and was put in the hospital. My father and sister came to get my children and I and bring us back home. I told my dad what I could remember and he said I was just overreacting. He saw no problem. I needed to work harder on the marriage and things would work out.

That was the beginning of PTSD for me. I couldn't figure out what I did wrong when all along it was my husband's anger and drinking problems. I was led to believe it was my fault because people don't understand PTSD. They would rather ignore it or pass it off as something else.

The last time my husband went to leave, I, again, tried to stop him. He almost killed me and put me in the hospital once again. I would say, "what did I do wrong? Is it my children? Do I push too much?". He would say, "I told you not to give me orders or cramp my space". I called the VA and they said they could do nothing unless the vet came into the hospital. Now this made a lot of sense because many vets are in denial, not thinking they have a problem. Thus, I was left out because he refused to get help from the VA. I was not eligible for any help myself as the spouse of a veteran.

We finally got divorced and I said never again would I have anything to do with a Vietnam vet. My children went through all this with me and, in their own way, suffered the consequences. I think this is how spouses and significant others develop the disease from the person with PTSD.

My third husband was not in the service. We were married for only five months. He couldn't deal with my children.

My fourth husband was in the Air Force. He was an ordnance officer. His job was to send and receive reports and orders dealing with the issuing of guns and equipment for the troops in Vietnam. He was also assigned to do the paperwork for those killed in action. After doing this for one year, he was sent back home to Fairchild Air Force Base in Spokane, Wa. There, he was doing the same type of work until he was reassigned to be the recreation officer.

He was married once before, however, their marriage did not work because of his anger and controlling issues. This was the beginning of psychiatric problems for him. He never went for help.

When we met, we were both shy of wanting a relationship. He told me he loved my kids and thought we would do well together. Knowing my children needed a father, I agreed to marry him. We talked about Vietnam and he told me, though he was there, he was not in combat. I thought okay, this is different, therefore we can make a go of it, not only for him but for my children and I. WRONG!

After about seven years, he developed a great deal of anger and control issues with my children and I. We talked about it and I asked if he felt he might need to go to counselling. He said no. His first wife and he had the same problems and it was that he needed to be in control and that's that. As his anger got out of control, he started yelling and hitting the walls, windows, the kids, and me. I had taken enough and told him if he didn't get help I would leave. He said the VA wouldn't do anything; that it wasn't a psychiatric problem, it was the world and the people in it. WRONG, AGAIN. I called the VA and got help for him and I in family groups. The counselors at the VA talked to both of us and said they might be able to help not only the marriage but also his psychiatric problems. He went to a couple of groups but then refused to go anymore. There was nothing else the VA could do.

After trying to solve our problems, the last straw was when he took a gun to my head and said if I left him he might as well kill me and himself because he had nothing left. I told him I would not go and that seemed to calm him down. I knew in my heart the marriage was over and I wanted to get away from him safely before I let him know I was getting a divorce. I didn't want to do it this way but I was afraid for the children and myself. I could not risk him taking a gun to them or me again. I moved to Seattle, Wa., and got a divorce. He never killed himself over it, however, he still has a lot of anger and control problems. The last I heard, he got into a relationship and now is getting treated for PTSD problems. I say, good for him, I hope it helps. I wish him the best.

My fifth husband, Tom, was in the Navy. He was a "brown water navy" gunner in the Mekong Delta in Vietnam. We are still married going on twenty-four years and now I will tell you about him. As you may guess, he has written Part One of this book. He is the love of my life and I will grow old with him.

Now, one would think enough is enough but NO, HERE I GO AGAIN falling in love with another Vietnam vet. Once again, I asked the question, "are you a vet? do you have problems with PTSD?". The answer was "no" because most vets will not tell you everything. They are afraid you will not go out with them because of the war and of being left behind. This is a big part of PTSD.

I was living in Seattle when I met Tom. I had transferred my job from Spokane to Seattle where I was an assistant manager of a restaurant working the night shift. One night, Tom came into the place and went into the cocktail lounge. I was in there pulling the money from the cash registers for the night. I told him he had to leave and to please come back some other time. After putting the money away, I went out to the restaurant section where Tom was seated at the counter. He asked, "can I buy you a cup of coffee?". We began to talk. He asked me if I had children as he never did. I told him I have five children and didn't want anymore. I thought this was strange but dismissed it because he was so nice to talk to and besides, he was so cute. We went out for almost a year without problems. He seemed to like my kids and they got along with him.

We started talking about getting married. I asked him about his family. He said his parents were killed in an auto accident and his brother had disappeared. I felt bad about this and I told him we are now his family. That seemed to please him. We set the date and got married on December 1st, 1984. It was a small wedding, only a few of his friends and co-workers came. Most all were betting that the marriage was not going to last. I should have clued into this at the time but passed it off. They knew Tom had a lot of anger and drug problems, therefore, they didn't see us staying married because I was not his type.

It wasn't until after we were married for about one year that I found out he, indeed, was in Vietnam. He had and still does have problems with PTSD. We talked about it and he told me he had been medi-vaced home from the war. His mother and father had come to see him in the naval hospital. He was there due to physical and battle fatigue problems. Tom was not diagnosed with PTSD until 1986. His mother had said, "that's not my son". She could not handle the battle fatigue part of Tom's hospitalization and walked out. Tom's dad, being a vet himself, should have tried to explain a few things to her but he just walked out with Tom's mother and never came back. Now this is enough to break anyone's heart. I thought how could anyone do that?

As I began to learn more about Tom, I felt once again trapped in the damn Vietnam War. What choices did I have? Do I go or stay and wonder what else will come up. I learned from Tom's grandmother that he had lied to me about his parents being dead. In fact, they were still alive and living in Portland, Or. He was ashamed that they had walked out on him, leaving him behind like he was nothing. I chose to stay and try to help Tom with his personal and PTSD problems. I told him if you seek help, I will stand by you forever. I believe, at that time, Tom felt he finally had someone who cared and it gave him hope.

As the years passed, both Tom and I were going to counselling and doing better. We learned by trial and error what each other can expect in life. This does not mean everything was fine. You still have outside issues like family, friends, and work to deal with which causes things to change as time goes on. Tom, as I had suspected, started having more problems with his PTSD and drugs after about two years into the marriage. He started drifting away. We began to fight and all the signs came back (by now, I knew in my mind I had developed PTSD of my own). The kids began to get on Tom's nerves. Pressures from my family, his work, and all the bills continued.

By 1986, Tom's depression, anger, and intrusive thoughts were getting out of control. Not knowing what to do, I went out one night with some of my close friends. I needed to talk with someone about what to do. Upon returning home, I found Tom very depressed and angry. I tried to talk to him but he withdrew from me. He went into the kitchen crying. I went to see if I could do anything for him. I made the mistake of trying to grab ahold of him. In an instant, he was back in Nam with a flashback that was caused by triggers. He thought I was a gook, grabbed a knife, and held me down against the sink. He told me, "don't move or I will kill you". I yelled to the kids to call 911 and go hide in their rooms. My oldest son was home from work and he made three calls to 911 before anyone came to help. Almost one hour had passed and Tom was getting closer to the no return point. This happens to a lot of vets with flashbacks. Sometimes they never come out of a flashback and live the rest of their lives in an institution or in the hills. Thank God, when the cops came, one was a Vietnam vet. He was able to calm Tom down and get the knife away from him. Tom was taken away to the hospital and sent to Tacoma, Wa., (please note, after our marriage, we had moved to Spokane). He was at the American Lake VA hospital for six months of in-patient care for PTSD.

I stood by him through all this, knowing in my heart he was a good man and I loved him. Years passed before problems began again. Tom started on drugs and booze due to his problems with depression, anger, anxiety, and intrusive thoughts, all components of PTSD. I finally left him for six months. I got an apartment with my youngest daughter. Tom and I would talk to each other and finally, I agreed to come back. He agreed to really try this time.

As more years passed, Tom kept his promises and got off drugs and booze. The children were all grown by now and have families of their own. Now, it was just Tom and I. He began to have more problems with his PTSD. The doctors said he could no longer work. We filed for one hundred per cent compensation for PTSD. After two government shutdowns and almost one year, we finally got it in April, 1996.

We have tried to cope with our PTSD problems in many ways. We go to groups, Tom talks with the doctors, and takes medication. We try to explain what PTSD is to family, friends, and anyone who cares to listen. We even tried to contact Tom's parents. I sent them letters and pictures of the kids and Tom and I. I was hoping against hope they would see him for this was truly a chapter in his life that needed to be closed. They still, after thirty years, wanted nothing to do with him. I know this must hurt him so much. I try to give him double the love and understanding. I talked with my family about this. My family was almost as bad as his. This is what happens to a veteran who has PTSD. The family does not take the time or the effort to try to understand all the side effects of PTSD. This is a sad country when people, especially family, go around with blinders and ear plugs on because they don't want to hear or read about something that scares them.

From my point of view, having been married to four different vets and having PTSD of my own, I have learned that if you don't understand something, don't walk away. Pick up a book on it or go ask questions of someone knowledgeable. Isn't the person you are wondering about worth it???

In this next area of Chapter Twelve, I will be touching on my health and self esteem. My self esteem is something that not only involves husbands with personality disorders or PTSD but my own form of PTSD. By this I mean my life growing up and my life as a wife and mother.

I grew up at the end of the depression and things were tough for my parents, as well as many people. My parents had to put my two sisters and I into foster homes until they could find jobs and get back on their feet. I can't tell you the horror this caused. I had one foster home parent who cut off all my hair and not feed me because I cried for my mother. This left me feeling angry and hopelessly depressed. My sisters and I had another foster parent who would not do anything. We had to do the cooking and the cleaning and were fed very little. This created a great deal of anger and depression for us. We couldn't understand why our parents could leave us with such mean people. Thus the feeling of being left behind.

When our parents finally got back on their feet, they came and took my two sisters with them. They took me to live with my aunt for a while. This again, had me feeling like I was being left behind causing more anxiety and anger. I never got over those feelings and, to this day, I am reminded of that at times, giving me a fear of not being wanted.

Given the above issues, I have developed PTSD. I have anger, anxiety, depression, and the left behind feelings. It is extremely difficult to deal with. On one hand, you want your spouse, family, and other people in your life but on the other hand, you pull away for fear of losing them in death or having them walk out of your life.

Years later, I still carry this baggage in my life. An example of this is retraced to my first husband. He left me for my best friend, hence the left behind and anger feelings. My second husband was the beater and the one who almost killed me. He left me for my best friend's sister, hence the fear, anger, and left behind issues again. My fourth husband gave me anger, anxiety, depression, and control issues. My fifth husband (whom I am still married to and love very dearly) brought to the table his PTSD problems, as well, which has enhanced my own problems.

Many times, people have asked me, "how do you do it? you must be a saint". I honestly am not sure how I have. I believe my PTSD has helped me to be stronger and more understanding. I know this sounds strange but I have lived with PTSD so long that I can handle a great deal more than most because I have been there.

As far as my PTSD is concerned, I have been seen by two different counselors. The first one was okay. She dealt with support and self esteem issues. I was happy to be able to talk with someone who was there for spouses and significant others. I thought perhaps I can get a handle on my own PTSD issues. We had ten ladies in my group, three of them were vets. I was comfortable talking with them. I became friends with one who had served in Vietnam. We would go to each other's house and sometimes go out to lunch. This lasted until she had a breakdown and left her husband. She stopped coming to groups and to see me. I was left feeling upset because I thought I had finally found a special friend I could talk to. After about two months, the group broke up due to the fact the VA no longer provided funding for it.

The second counselor was through the Disabled American Veterans. She was ineffective because she didn't know much about PTSD. This lady would talk to everyone on a one to one basis and have a group once a week. I was having many problems at this time. I would tell her I thought my PTSD was getting to me and I didn't know how much more I could take. I felt so depressed and overwhelmed with Tom's problems as well as my own. Sometimes, I had suicidal thoughts. My family didn't understand Tom or I. I didn't know who to turn to. The counselor would say things like, "you must take care of yourself and let Tom take care of his own problems". RIGHT! She advised me to go to a camp for women of domestic violence and sort things out in my mind again. Sure, who has the money and can take time from work and family to go to places like that? Her final words of wisdom were, "then, get a divorce". That was unacceptable and uncalled for. I never went back to her.

There is not much help out there for the spouses and significant others of veterans with PTSD. Nor is there much help for the veteran. I believe this lack of assistance for our returning vets has caused a huge injustice to all involved. To me, this is why there are so many divorces and suicides. Again I say, "SHAME ON YOU, UNCLE SAM".

Chapter Thirteen

The Battle as a Whole

In this chapter, I will be talking about drug use, mind control issues, break up, and, sometimes a disruptive home life. These are the areas that were the most troubling in my marriage to Tom. As you read through my experiences, you should keep in mind that not all PTSD vets will go through these areas. For those who do, you, as the spouse or significant other, need to get information about them and seek counselling early on. If you truly love and care for the person, you will come out a winner in your battles.

Drug use was the most difficult area for me. It causes so much hurt, depression, fear, and financial problems. I noticed Tom's problem with drugs about three years into our marriage. I talked to him as to how I felt about drugs. As anyone on drugs will say, "don't worry about it, I can control it and I can quit anytime". I believed in him, not realizing the extent of his usage.

As the years went on, I became more concerned about the drug use. I hated what it was doing to Tom and to our family, as well. The drug use destroyed nearly everything good about our life together. I would tell Tom to please stop. I know you are doing more drugs; your attitude and behavior have changed so much. Like so many people on drugs, they can't see the problem until it's too late.

I saw several signs of Tom's usage. He would distance himself from the family and I. He would spend more time away from home. His personality went downhill and sometimes turned aggressive. Tom's dress code changed from very meticulous to just so so. He would sleep a lot and when awake, his eyes were dilated and cloudy. He became very protective of his personal belongings. He was no longer romantic. Money was a real issue with him. His appetite diminished significantly.

Finally, I had taken enough. I had been so deeply hurt and lost so much faith that I left Tom. As I think back to those six months while I was gone, I believe it brought us more closely together. During that time, we were able to talk and both of us learned a great deal about each other from that short separation.

Tom was able to get off drugs by himself. He knew he did it not only for himself but for me as well. Tom knew the choices were my love or his drug use. I was glad he chose me and I knew whatever it took, I would always stand by him. Tom is now drug free except for, obviously, his prescriptions. Sometimes though, I think he wants the release from regular life and to go back to them but he stays away. He knows my stand and it's me he wants to walk with down that rough and rocky road to the end of the construction. It was a hard battle but one I can say, "I WON!".

Mind control issues can be a large part of PTSD. An example of these is based on Tom's lonliness problems and feelings of being left behind. For instance, Tom will tell me to spend more time with my family. However, because of his problems he really doesn't want me to leave. He has the fear that something will happen to me whereby I won't return home. Due to Tom's lonliness, he displays a controlling behavior pattern. By this, I do not infer that he controls money issues, what I wear, or people that I see. It's that he wants me with him almost all the time. Sometimes he gets angry if I am gone too long or leave too much. Consequently, I feel guilty about doing anything outside the house without him. If Tom was more involved with activities or had friends, I feel his problems of feeling left behind would diminish.

I feel somewhat guilty for having family, friends, and activities because Tom actually has no one except me. Although my children do love and accept him, they do not know how to approach Tom due to his mood swings with PTSD. I tell him my family is his but I feel he has trouble accepting this. I believe this stems from his losses during the war, as well as, the loss of his parents and brother. I believe Tom fears any relationship will result in loss.

Chapter Fourteen

Winning the Battles

At this time of my life, I believe my personal symptoms and understanding of PTSD are beginning to level off. I feel I have more knowledge of the many forms of PTSD. These forms can be caused by war, abuse, auto accidents, fearfulness, rape, and the loss of someone close to you. Additionally, the signs of PTSD you may observe in yourself or someone else are:

1. Isolation
2. Bitterness
3. Depression
4. Nightmares
5. Intrusive Thoughts
6. Blame
7. Irritability
8. Anger
9. Conflict
10. Futility
11. Fear
12. Guilt
13. Shame
14. Frustration
15. Anxiety
16. Failure
17. Hopelessness
18. Aggressiveness
19. Sadness
20. Regret

I know in my heart, if you take the time to really understand what PTSD is, you will probably avoid many emotional and physical problems. I know that if I had done so early on, I would have been much better off.

The years have taken a toll on my health. My heart is not very good and I have high blood pressure. However, with medications from my doctor I am doing much better.

The doctors at the VA who see my husband have been very helpful in giving me advice and to steer me in the right direction.

Both Tom and I continue to battle PTSD problems but we are in better control now. During our struggles, we have found the following to be helpful:

1) *Trust* in each other
2) *Love* unconditionally
3) Listen to each other with *open minds*
4) Seek *information* about PTSD and *read it together*
5) Express your *concerns* with family and friends
6) Get *away* to a park or ocean beach where you can be *uninterrupted*
7) Show *affection* with your spouse or significant other

A very important concept is to find the *right doctor* who knows about PTSD and takes the time to discuss it with you. This may entail seeing several doctors before finding the one you are most *comfortable* with. Do not settle for a doctor whose only ambition appears to be to push *pills*. It is equally as important to find a therapist whom you can discuss your problems with.

There are outlets where you can go to seek help for PTSD. If you are a veteran, we suggest you go to a VA hospital mental hygiene unit for help. Normally, you will first see a regular doctor to discuss your symptoms (refer to the beginning of this chapter where "signs to look for" are listed). Insist that this doctor refer you to a psychiatrist who is knowledgeable about PTSD. It is vital that you be assertive about this and not let yourself be pushed around. Keep in mind, a psychiatrist who prescribes medication is important but you will also need someone with whom you can discuss your problems.

Other sources for consultation about PTSD for both veterans and non-veterans would be mental health outreach centers, local churches, private counselors, and other hospitals that have out-patient mental health clinics. All of the above may be free or on a sliding scale fee basis.

Other outlets for assistance are the military service organizations such as the Disabled American Veterans and the Veterans of Foreign Wars. They will assist you with the paperwork for filing disability claims with the VA.

An important source of intervention for anyone with PTSD is *group counselling*. You may have to go to a few different types of groups before you find the one that fits *your* needs. To be effective, a group *must* have a facilitator *proficient* in PTSD. Remember to check out the group *members* as well. Stay clear of those who only want to be involved in *gripe sessions*. You must have a *solidly structured* group to be effective.

Conclusion

In summing up Part Two of this book, I would like to offer my deepest gratitude to my children, other family members, friends, and mostly, my wonderful husband, Tom, for understanding my issues with PTSD. All the rough and bumpy roads of construction are beginning to smooth out.

I would like to acknowledge how difficult it was to write this book, not only for myself but for Tom as well. Writing this has caused Tom to go back in time and bring out many ghosts that previously had been laid to rest. We strongly feel that if it helps even one person, it certainly has been worth it.

Tom has gone through a great deal in his life, getting out of high school and off to Vietnam and the killing fields. He came home to his parents and brother not wanting anything to do with him. He also went through a bad first marriage, all of these due to PTSD problems. It has been a long battle with the VA and his cries for help going unanswered for a good length of time.

I can truly say after all these years, Tom has found someone, namely me, who cares. I found that by standing with him and learning about PTSD, I have come to grips with my life and can breathe a little easier now. There still will be rough times ahead for Tom and I but together we will overcome them with our love to keep us strong.

We wish all who read this book the best in their lives. Our hearts and prayers go out to all in your struggles with PTSD. Remember, you can learn to live with this disease.